Step Up to That New Career

Empower your life with a truly comprehensive approach to changing your career for a fresh start toward a better future.

Copyright and Permissions

All copyrights in this work are held by Richard A. Gunderson the author and owner of Career Job Transition LLC. As a customer, you are permitted to print one (1) hard copy of the work for your own personal use. Such printing may be done by a commercial printer and permission is hereby given to commercial printers to print the work for the purposes set forth herein.

Copyright © 2022 Richard A. Gunderson
All Rights Reserved
ISBN-9798428005066

Limits of Liability / Disclaimer of Warranty

The author and publisher of this book and any accompanying materials have used their best efforts in preparing this book. The author and publisher make no representation or warranties with respect to accuracy, applicability, fitness, or completeness of the contents of this program. They disclaim any warranties (expressed or implied), merchantability, or fitness for any particular purpose. The author and publisher shall in no event be held liable for any loss or other damages, including but not limited to special, incidental, consequential, or other damages. As always, the advice of a competent legal, tax, accounting, or other professional should be sought. The author and publisher do not warrant the performance, effectiveness, or applicability of any sites listed in this book. All links are for information purposes only and are not warranted for content, accuracy, or any other implied or explicit purpose.

This document contains material protected under International and Federal Copyright Laws and Treaties. Any unauthorized reprint or use of this material is prohibited.

Dedication

I dedicate this eBook to my late wife Marie Raese Gunderson. Marie and I met our first week at Taylor University. We dated most of our four years until graduation. Upon graduating we were married in Grosse Pointe Michigan. After a short honeymoon we settled in an apartment in New Brighton, Minnesota. Marie taught in an elementary school. She was a wonderful 5th grade teacher, and she loved her students. Marie was a loving, supportive, and devoted wife. We were partners in a marriage that lasted until she passed away from a heart attack. She is the mother of our two daughters Cheri Lynn Mueller and Susan Marie Karrmann. We all miss her. She loved the Lord and I have no doubt that I will see her in heaven. Marie was a humble person. I never fully realized the positive impact that she had on people until after she passed away when many of her friends shared stories about their relationship. Marie had a positive impact on me, her husband. She often coached me in my writing. It was with her support that in early 2017 I began training and coaching unemployed professionals in search of new employment. To her credit, I continue in that work today.

Acknowledgements

My name is Richard Gunderson. In early 2017, I began training and coaching professionals (i.e., salaried exempt employees). I want to thank Stephen Withrow, John Englund, Bud Becker, Lonny Gulden, Earl Johnson, and the Job Transition Support Group at Wooddale Church. Each of them in their own way were excellent examples and sources of wisdom that were beneficial to me.

Prior to the pandemic I trained about 1,000 professionals and I provided about 150 with one-on-one coaching. I learned a great deal from these men and women through their open and honest communication for which I am grateful. They were earnest as they pursued new employment opportunities. Many of them wanted to step up to that new career or they wanted a new professional job in a similar line of work. What a blessing to see them moving forward to a brighter future with a focus on securing the employment they desired.

Table of Contents

Copyright & Permissions
Limits of Liability / Disclaimer of Warranty
Dedication
Acknowledgements
Introduction
Chapter One – Begin With the End in Mind
Chapter Two – The Benefit of a Career Change
Chapter Three - Assessing Your Value
Chapter Four – Story Telling
Chapter Five – Career Consideration
Chapter Six – Relationship Building
Chapter Seven – Marketing Plan
Chapter Eight – Marketing Action
Chapter Nine – Resume Customization
Chapter Ten – Cover Letter Writing
Chapter Eleven – Management Interviewing
Chapter Twelve – Interview Follow-Up
About the Author
Wrap Up

Introduction

This book was written to provide professional men and women like you with guidance that will enable you to effectively step up to that new career opportunity or the possibility of new professional job in a similar line of work with confidence.

Written by an expert on job transition and career change, this book is written for professional men and women from their early twenties to their mid sixties regardless of their career, areas of excellence, unique talents, years of experience, or current title. They are unique individuals with unique needs. When it comes to their pursuit of employment opportunities, the comprehensive approach to job search described in detail in this book addresses most of those unique needs. The author is willing to address specific issues via email support.

Relevant scripture verses are sprinkled throughout this book to keep employment search in proper perspective.

If you wanted a career with a fresh start, my desire is that you will step up to that new career and open the door to a better future for you and your family.

Chapter 1 – Keep The End in Mind

Charles Lutwidge Dodgson, better known by his pen name Lewis Carroll, was an English author, illustrator, poet, mathematician, photographer, teacher, and inventor. He is remembered for his work "Alice's Adventures in Wonderland" written in 1865. An exchange between Alice and the Cheshire Cat goes like this: :

Alice: *"Would you tell me, please, which way I ought to go from here?"*

The Cat: *"That depends a good deal on where you want to get to."*

Alice: *"I don't much care where."*

The Cat: *"Then it doesn't matter which way you go"*

Alice: *"…..so long as I get SOMEWHERE.".*

The Cat: *"Oh, you're sure to do that, if you only walk long enough."*

Little did the author know that he was describing the approach many professionals take in their search for new employment. They just begin trying a bunch of things, like rewriting their resume or scheduling interviews, without a clear understanding of what they are looking for and where they are going. Without a direction, without a goal, without knowing where you're going, is all the same. You end up going nowhere, you never get there, and you can never arrive anywhere because you don't have a destination. With a little luck you will get somewhere, but what will you find and how long will it take?

Dr. Stephen Covey wrote "The Seven Habits of Highly Effective People". Habit #2 says "begin with the end in mind".

He described it as *"being based on imagination. the ability to envision in your mind what you cannot at present see with your eyes. It is based on the principle that all things are created twice. There is a mental (first) creation, and a physical (second) creation. The physical creation follows the mental, just as a building follows a blueprint."*

"If you don't make a conscious effort to visualize who you are and what you want in life, then you empower other people and circumstances to shape you and your life by default. It's about connecting again with your uniqueness and then defining the personal, moral, and ethical guidelines within which you can most happily express and fulfill yourself."

"One of the best ways to incorporate Habit 2 into your life is to develop a personal mission statement. It focuses on what you want to be and do. It is your plan for success. It reaffirms who you are, puts your goals in focus, and moves your ideas into the real world. Your mission statement makes you the leader of your own life. You create your destiny and secure the future you envision."

In this book you'll be asked to develop a value proposition that describers the qualities and value you can offer a potential employer. But before we get there, visualize three things that describe what you desire for your next career:
1. Job Fit
2. Culture
3. Work Environment

By visualizing at the start of your employment search you will do as Stephen Covey says, "it puts your goals in focus, and moves your ideas into the real world. Your mission statement makes you the leader of your own life. You create your destiny and secure the future you visualize.

Job Fit

Organizational psychologists typically define "fit" in two different ways,

- Person-job fit is generally the most common. It identifies a candidate's suitability for tasks required to succeed in a specific job. This can include their skills, knowledge levels, strengths, and abilities.
- Person-organization fit refers to a match between an organization's core values and culture and an individual's beliefs and values.

Person-Job Fit

"Person-job fit is important for your work because it has strong implications for your well-being.

- *It impacts job satisfaction, as well as satisfaction with your coworkers and supervisor.*
- *You can also expect increases in your organizational commitment and identification when you fit well with your job.*
- *Finally, your strain decreases when you fit better with your job. So, overall, you'll be happier, more dedicated to your organization, and less stressed when you fit better with your job."*
- *"In addition to increasing well-being, person-job fit has other positive implications for organizations. Because person-job fit increases your attitude, it can also enhance your performance. It makes sense that your performance might increase when you are better suited toward your job. Also, fitting better to your job can also decrease the likelihood that you want to leave. So, you're less likely to*

turn over in the long run when you feel you fit well with your job."

Culture

Glassdoor's November 2019 survey results that relate to a person-organization fit:

- *When searching for a new job, 77% of respondents said they would consider a company's culture before applying.*
- *American millennials are more likely to care about work culture over salary (65%) than those age 45 and older (52%). Similar numbers were found in the U.K. (66% vs. 52%).*
- *89% of adults polled told researchers that it was important for employers to "have a clear mission and purpose."*

"A common misperception among many employers today is that pay and work-life balance are among the top factors driving employee satisfaction," said Dr. Andrew Chamberlain, Glassdoor's chief economist. "*We find little support for this notion in Glassdoor data. Instead, employers looking to boost hiring and employee retention efforts should prioritize building strong company culture and value systems, amplifying the quality and visibility of their senior leadership teams and offering clear, exciting career opportunities to employees.*"

Five factors to consider in evaluating a company culture:
1. Evaluate the onboarding process – Do they provide the training, resources, and tools new employees need?
2. Gauge openness with leadership
3. Look at incentive programs (or lack thereof)
4. Observe team interactions
5. Determine attitudes from answers

Work Environment

"A work environment refers to the elements that comprise the setting in which employees work and impact workers. While some items that comprise it are obvious, such as the wall treatment or the number of indoor plants, others are more obtuse, such as company politics or a coworker whose personality traits do not suit the company culture. Professionals working in both full-time and part-time positions are significantly impacted by their office environment because they have to perform their duties inside it. Usually, workers are required to adapt to this workplace feature."

The following list will help you to look for symptoms of the work environment at a potential employer. The work environment is important because:

- *It can involve better conditions for workers, which can improve loyalty and build the corporate brand.*
- *It can increase employee satisfaction, motivation, and engagement.*
- *It can increase the productivity of workers who are eager to contribute to the company.*
- *It can avoid creating conditions in which the workers are dissatisfied or demotivated.*
- *It can make it easier to identify issues in the environment, such as an adversarial worker who reduces morale.*
- *It can include managers who use positive reinforcement to build employee satisfaction and engagement.*

- *It can include workers who treat others with respect and empathy.*
- *It can avoid distractions that prevent workers from performing their job responsibilities.*
- *It can support communication between workers from different occupations and levels of the company.*
- *It can generate many opportunities for professional growth through items such as internal promotions or training programs.*
- *It can encourage positive thinking among workers through employer programs, visual details in the physical setting, and worker-friendly policies.*
- *It can promote a work-life balance for both supervisors and subordinates.*

Summary

In your desire to step up to that new career, or new professional role you wanted, or new job role for women over fifty, have you stopped to consider where you want to go with your career? Have you thought through what you want it to look like when you get there? Hopefully you will consider these factors early in the employment search process. Having these factors in mind at the start of the search, will influence your thinking throughout the search.

One of the major challenges that professionals face is in establishing specific career goals. This is often the case with professionals that have been in the workplace for 10 or more years. They've often held a variety of positions in different roles. Upon leaving an organization they may find it difficult to decide which career path to follow. It's important to make that decision as soon as possible. Without clarity on that one point, a lack of focus will often be evident to others in networking meetings and interviews. That can hurt your chances of being selected for that ideal job you are pursuing.

Chapter 2 – The Benefit of a Career Change

Could it be that you wanted a career with a fresh start? A fresh start sounds good. But why?
- There are many good reasons for pursuing a career change at any age.
- Circumstances often pile up causing a person to want to get a fresh start in a new career.
- There are many reasons to play it safe and not pursue a career change.

You may recognize that: transitioning from unemployment into a new career is scary. Leaving the security of an existing job may be a big risk. This eBook will provide you with:
- Reasons for making a career change.
- Pros and cons worthy of consideration.
- References to helpful resources.
- A proven process for securing a new career at any age with guided steps to a brighter career.
- Information career change men over 50 need to know.
- Step-by-step guidance in how to secure a new job role for women over fifty.
- A biblical perspective to provide direction and comfort for you at this stage of life.

Did you know that the Bible talks about fresh starts? In The Message paraphrase of the Bible, we find several references to "fresh start"
- Zachariah 10:6 (The Message) reads *"I'll save the people of Joseph. I know their pain and will make them good as new. They'll get a fresh start."*
- Hosea 14:5 *"I will make a fresh start with Israel. They'll burst into bloom like a crocus in the spring."*
- Psalm 145:14 *"God gives a hand to those down on their luck, gives a fresh start to those ready to quit."*

Reverend Rick Warren (author of "The Purpose Driven Life") says that *"God is the God of second chances. The God of new beginnings. The God of starting over. The God of giving people a fresh start."*

- If you were to ask God for a fresh start, what would that look like for you?
- Are you willing to act in pursuit of a God-given dream, your second chance?
- Are you ready to get started? When?

Chapter 3 – Assessing Your Value

> **ROMANS 12:3** (NLT): *"Don't think you are better than you really are. Be honest in your evaluation of yourselves, measuring yourselves by the faith God has given us."*
> **PROVERBS 15:22** (The Message): *"Refuse good advice and watch your plans fail .... take good counsel and watch them succeed."*
> **PROVERBS 18:15** (NLT): *"Intelligent people are always ready to learn. Their ears are open for knowledge."*

Now that you've developed a vision with the end in mind (Chapter 1) and you have the sense for the fresh start that a new career can offer (Chapter 2) it's time to start with Step One in the ten-step employment search process. That might cause you to think this is a lengthy time-consuming process, but it isn't. Most people that follow this process find that it provides focus and efficiency that will produce results (i.e., job offers) in a relatively short time.

Your situation is likely described by one of these three statements:

- Currently employed but unhappy. It's not the right fit and you're looking to step up to that new career, or maybe you wanted a new professional job in a similar line of work.
- You are currently unemployed because your employment was terminated by your employer or voluntarily by you.
- You took a long-term leave of absence and are now ready to re-enter the workforce.

- You're looking for guided steps to a brighter career. That's somewhat obvious because you're reading this book.

Regardless of your situation, you should always start here in Step One. I know from experience that it's tempting to jump into the process at some later stage like writing or updating a resume. Too many job seekers learn the hard way that this is a mistake that may cause the transition to take longer.

When you're ready to consider assessing your value the question is "what should you assess?" Employers will be looking to hire someone when they have a problem that needs to be solved. They'll make a job offer when a candidate can convince them that they can solve that problem or making a significant contribution to solving that problem.

What are employers looking for? Here are nine attributes representing what an employer is likely going to want to know.
1. Attitude
2. Skills
3. Strengths
4. Passion
5. Personality
6. Reputation
7. Unique Talents
8. Employment Goals
9. The Job Fit

When looking at the above list, it seems that this step is all about "self-assessment". That it is. But more importantly, you should never lose site of the fact that in the end "It's Not About You". Keep in mind that you're trying to land a job in which the employer has a need.

- The employer will establish their priorities in searching for the right candidate.
- The employer will decide which candidate is best suited to meet their needs (not the employee's needs)

I encourage you to document your thoughts as you go through each of these topics.

Attitude

Whenever employment is terminated, it is common that there had been feelings of dissatisfaction on the part of the employer, or the employee, or the organization fell on hard times and had to reduce overhead cost that often means reducing employee headcount.

A 2019 report indicated that *"80% of workers are either actively looking for a new job or are open to one."* That same report indicated that
- *"one-third of job seekers left a job within 90 days;*
- *43% of that group said their day-to-day role wasn't what they thought it would be;*
- *34% said they were driven away by a bad experience or incident; and*
- *32% cited company culture."*

The above data points to an employee that has had a bad experience resulting in a negative attitude.

If your last job was terminated, you experienced the psychological impact of that termination. A Gallup poll indicated *"the longer that Americans are unemployed, the more likely they are to report signs of poor psychological well-being. About one in five Americans who have been unemployed for a year or more say they currently have or are being treated for depression – almost double the rate among those who have been unemployed for five weeks or less."* That same poll indicated that *"the loss of hope that can accompany long-term unemployment may be detrimental not only to job seekers' quality of life, but also to their ability to find good jobs."*

<u>Which of these attitudes apply to you?</u>
- ☐ Frustration
- ☐ Confusion
- ☐ Sense of Loss
- ☐ Self Confidence Lost
- ☐ Financial Fears
- ☐ Discouragement
- ☐ Embarrassment

☐ Depression

If you are experiencing some level of depression, please seek the help of a professional counsellor or therapist that can help.

<u>Let Go of Negativity</u>:

Whether you look at life from a negative perspective or positive perspective, it's a choice.
- Negative thinking will never make your life positive.
- When in a job search, letting go of negativity will positively impact your life, reduce your stress, and enable you to present a positive impression when in the middle of an interview.
- A person that chooses to dwell on the negative is often a loner because positive people tend to avoid negative people.
- You are vulnerable when you are alone.

A quote from the Bible: Ecclesiastes 4:10 says; *"If one person falls, the other can reach out and help. But someone who falls alone is in real trouble."*
- You need relationships with others for encouragement, refreshment, and growth during your job search.
- Accept help but keep your eyes open to others that you could encourage.
- Positive relationships and the opportunity to encourage others will reduce stress in your own life.

Skills

It's important that you are aware of your skills. Employers put a priority on skills, and they will identify the skills they are looking for when they open a position to be filled. There are three types of skills:
- Hard skills
- Soft skills
- Transferrable skills (this will be covered in Step Three)

Hard Skills:

Hard skills are also referred to as "learned skills". They may be skills that you learned in school, or skills that you learned on-the-job. Another characteristic of hard skills is that they are relatively easy to measure. Examples of hard skills include:

- Typing/Keyboarding
- Word processing
- Computer programming
- Mathematics
- Surgery
- Statistics
- Website design/development
- Video editing
- Graphic design
- Accounting
- Economics
- Marketing
- Cloud and Distributed Computing
- Engineering (Electrical, Electronic, Mechanical, Civil, Aeronautical)

Make a list of the hard skills that you have mastered (not the ones you wish you had mastered).

Which of these are hard skills?

- ☐ Photography
- ☐ Conflict Management
- ☐ Cybersecurity
- ☐ Foreign language
- ☐ Persuasion

Soft Skills:

Soft skills are also referred to as "people skills" or "interpersonal skills". They are difficult to measure. This is a partial list of soft skills:

- Flexibility
- Leadership
- Motivation
- Resilience
- Patience
- Confidence
- Mutual Respect
- Problem Solving
- Delegation
- Presentation Skills
- Mediation
- Creativity
- Tolerance
- Questioning
- Leadership
- Humor

Which of these are soft skills?
- ☐ Introspection
- ☐ Adaptability
- ☐ Communication
- ☐ Teamwork
- ☐ Persuasion

Strengths

The CliftonStrengths assessment is a performance-based tool that builds self-awareness. Unlike personality tests, it goes beyond general definitions of your personal traits and digs into how specific strengths can be cultivated. It helps individuals discover their top five strengths.

You've likely heard of personality tests like Myers-Briggs. Personality tests can be useful in helping you gain awareness, but many people have a hard time applying the information they receive. They offer generalized feedback, like whether you're introverted or extroverted.

The CliftonStrengths assessment provides detailed information about each characteristic. This helps you uncover the areas where you have the greatest potential for building your strengths. Over 90% of Fortune 500 companies have used this assessment.

Click here to take the assessment quiz and learn your Top Five Clifton Strengths. It will cost you around $20 to take the assessment, but it is worth the investment.

Employer Preference Skills Inventory:

You're not ready to get serious about a specific employer, but you probably have an idea what you'd like to do in terms of your career moving forward. It might be helpful to identify a job title that is a good fit for you.

1. Pick a title that might fit your career goals.
2. Go to www.indeed.com
3. Enter the job title
4. Enter the location (optional)
5. Look through some of the job postings. Find 5 that look interesting. Print a copy of each of those 5 job postings.
6. Highlight each hard skill and soft skill you see in each of the five postings.
7. Create a table that looks like the table below but with 7 columns. Add more rows if you prefer to assess more than five employers.
8. Enter the name of each unique skill you identified in #6 above in the left-hand column of the table. (Do not enter the same skill twice).
9. Enter the employer's name at the top of the column labeled #1. In that column put a check mark to the right of the name of the skill if that skill applies to you.
10. Repeat for job postings #2, #3, #4, and #5. Total the number of checks in each row.

Soft Skill	#1	#2	Total

Once you've analyzed all five job postings and entered check marks in the table, look at the results.
- Do you have a lot of check marks?
- Are there certain skills those 5 employers consider important that you are qualified for?
- What do the totals in the right-hand column tell you about whether you are the right person for a position with this job title?
- Do you need to consider an alternate job title?

Note: You will not meet all the requirements for any position. But you should meet many of the requirements if that job title is the right role for you.

Passion

Passion is about emotions, the motivation and what makes you feel good (i.e., do what you love). Purpose is the reason, or the why behind what you do, primarily for others.

Passionate employees are often happier and more productive because they enjoy the work they do. They look forward to going to work most days. **Action**: Develop thoughts about your passion and how it relates to your career.

Your passion should be evident in your communication and marketing materials.

Action: Identify examples of how you've pursued this passion in the past.

Steve Jobs quote: *"The only way to do great work, love what you do."*

Richard Branson quote: *"There is no greater thing you can do with your life and your work than follow your passions in a way that serves the world and you."*

Question: Did you find passion in a previous employment? Does your vision for the future cause you to be ready to step up to that new career and find passion in that employment?

Document your thoughts about passion and save it for later steps in the ten-step process.

Personality

Historically, hiring decisions were heavily based on experience and skills. According to a study, 70% of employers consider personality to be among the top three factors in their decision whether to extend a job offer.
- Confidence is in second place.
- Authenticity, honesty, reliability, and self-discipline are about equal in third place.
- Arrogance or overconfidence is a huge turn-off.

Question: How will you demonstrate your personality to a Hiring Manager?

Reputation

Your reputation can be helped or hindered by social media content. Employers reject as many as 25% of applicants because of social-media content. That includes:
- Alcohol
- Substance consumption
- Comments
- Offensive comments
- Inappropriate photos

Remember, what you think of your social media content is not what's important. It's what a prospective employer thinks about your social media content that is important. Your online presence is your digital brand. Ask yourself......
- "What happens in Vegas" seldom "stays in Vegas.". What happened in Vegas that you would not want a prospective employer to know?
- Is your LinkedIn profile up to date?
- What does your frequency of online activity say about you?
- Is your messaging consistent with what you want employers to know about you?

Unique Talents

> **I Peter 4:10** (the Living Bible): *"God has given each of you some special abilities; be sure to use them to help each other, passing on to others God's many kinds of blessings."*

What do you have that few people you've met in your industry have? Whether you believe it or not, you have something special. Answer these questions:
- What makes you unique?
- What were your three biggest accomplishments in the past 3 years?
- What three words describe how you were able to accomplish/solve the biggest problem you faced in your most recent employment?

This is not a time to be shy or humble. At the same time be honest.

Employment Goals

The work you've done and the thoughts you've been processing in Step One should help you in formulating your employment goals.

Question: How many different employment goals are you considering?

At this early stage in the job transition training, it's okay that you have more than one employment goal in mind. But three is too many.
- Keep in mind that you're eventually going to have to explain your career goals to a Hiring Manager.

- Hiring Managers will be looking for you to demonstrate clear concise focus on your future plans. That means one and only one employment goal.
- Be prepared to narrow your focus soon.

The Job Fit

Job fit is a concept that refers to how well an employee is suited for his or her position.
When an employee is a good fit for a job, they are more likely willing to remain an employee of the company.
When employees are well-suited for their positions, they are happier and more productive.
A 2019 report indicated that "a third of job seekers left a job within 90 days; 43% of that group said their day-to-day role wasn't what they thought it would be; 34% said they were drive away by a bad experience or incident; and 32% cited company culture."

Questions To Ponder

1. Why do you think Assessing Your Value is Step One in the career transition process?
2. What do you consider your strength now that you've gone through this Assessment step?
3. What surprised you about yourself when going through this Assessment?
4. What is going to be your biggest concern as you go through this transition process?

Throughout this ten-step career transition process training, ten secrets will be presented that need to be clearly understood in your mind. Following is Secret #1.

Secret #1

It's Never About You

Keep your mind focused on the potential employer. What is it that they need? Without that information, you don't have a story to tell.

Chapter Summary

The information disclosed in this chapter lays a foundation for future work you'll be doing in communicating your skills, strengths, character, and goals. You won't be communicating all the information covered in this chapter. All communication must be specific to the needs and concerns of a potential employer. Each employer will have their own unique concerns. So, assessment on a broader scale will be helpful.

Keep in mind, that the employment search is "not about you". It is about the employer's problems and their desire to hire people that can make a difference for their organization in ways that are unique to them.

Periodically review the thoughts you've documented on each of these eight topics. You'll likely be asked questions pertaining to many of them.

Chapter 4 – Story Telling

> **PSALM 78:4** (The Message): *"Listen dear friends, to God's truth. Bend your ears to what I tell you. I'll let you in on the sweet old truths. Stories we heard from our fathers. Counsel we learned at our mother's knee. We're not keeping this to ourselves. We're passing it along to the next generation ...God's fame and fortune, the marvelous things he has done."*

Chapter 4 (Step Two in the ten-step Process) focuses on:
- The importance of story telling in your search for new employment.
- How to write your stories.
- How to communicate those stories.
- When to communicate those stories.

If you were introduced to a stranger and he/she asked you "who are you?" Would you be prepared with an answer? Or would you mentally stumble around trying to come up with an intelligent answer?

If the person asking the question potentially held the keys to a job that you might be interested in, it would be good if your story said something about what you wanted to do in the future and why that was important to you.

When you tell a story. . ..
- You open lines of communication
- You open doors of opportunity
- You reveal important information
- The message is memorable

It would be great if the story was delivered spontaneously. Impressive if delivered naturally.

Accomplishments

In the middle of your search for new employment, communication is extremely important. One of the most important elements in communication is the relevance of the information about your past including accomplishments, disappointments, and what you learned from them.

<u>What makes an accomplishment relevant?</u>
If you are going to provide relevant information, then you need to start by asking some questions of the other party to determine who they are and what is important to them. Without that information, you're unable to identify relevance to what you're about to communicate. Once you've identified relevance in your own mind, then you are prepared to communicate a relevant accomplishment.

In most cases an accomplishment is an expression of work-related results. Communicate the following:
- How the accomplishment was a benefit to a previous employer
- An accurate message about your role in the story
- The accomplishment demonstrates a result that is pertinent to a potential employer
- It includes the use of metrics. How big were the results? How much was accomplished?

You want to step up to that new career. One way to make that happen is to demonstrate how you stepped up and made a difference to a previous employer. Your metrics will help sell your story.

<u>Examples of metrics</u>
Metrics that are most likely common to both a past employer and a potential employer are the major items like:
- Sales – increased sales by 5%
- Profit (net income) – profits increased by 7%
- Downtime – system downtime decreased from 1% to 0.4%

- Injuries – work related injuries were reduced by 50%
- Fund Raising – Increased fund-raising year-over-year by 10%

Whenever you can demonstrate results with metrics, you have a strong message to tell and an easier message to understand.

Completing a project is not an accomplishment.

What if you have accomplishments but no metrics?

- There are roles in every organization where results were not available. If that's the case, click on this link: https://www.jobscan.co/blog/dont-need-numbers-accomplishments-resume/

STAR Stories

One of the most effective ways to communicate a story that is relevant in your search for new employment is in the form of a STAR story. A STAR story will be very effective in making it possible for you to step up to that new career. A STAR story can be embedded in a resume, a cover letter, and can be used very effectively in an interview.

You're not ready to make use of your STAR stories. That will come later in this ten-step process. But you'll be ahead of the game if you write your STAR stories now.

STAR is an acronym. The letters and what they stand for are as follows:

S – Situation: A simple statement declaring where you were, where you worked, and in what capacity.

T – Task: A statement of your specific duty or goal during the event/situation.

A – Action: How you were involved. What you did. What others did. Why you took these actions.

R- Result: A description of the tangible outcomes and how they impacted your employer. (Be specific, avoid vague statements)

Example of a Situation:
A potential customer asked our organization to customize one of our products to incorporate some unique features that we had never designed before. Our staff had no knowledge of how to design these features.

Example of a Task:
The challenge was to identify the total set of customer needs, available technology, and alternative approaches to design these unique features into our product.

Example of an Action:
I took responsibility for working with one of our marketing team members and the customer to develop a more in-depth understanding of what they were looking for, how it was to function for their customer, and acceptable limits on the incremental cost of producing our product with these unique features.

With this information, I put together a small team of design, marketing, and manufacturing staff within our company to consider alternative technical and manufacturing solutions that would meet the customer's needs.

Example of a Result:

I provided the management leadership for our team to identify two design approaches that came closest to meeting the customer's needs. We reviewed the two approaches with the customer and selected one that would meet their needs at acceptable incremental cost to the customer. Because of our work we received a big contract for a version of our product with these unique features. We were also able to get a patent on the intellectual property rights for the product. This led to future contracts that increased our sales revenue by an average of 15% over the first three years. It also increased sales revenue for our customer.

Difficulty in writing a STAR story

STAR stories are difficult to write. I recommend you start writing your first STAR story in response to the following question: *Tell me about your biggest accomplishment to date.*

Because you're usually writing stories about accomplishments related to work done for a previous employer, it may be difficult to reconstruct the full STAR story. But it will be worth the effort.

How many stories should you write?

- How many organizations are you going to connect with?
- How many organizations will schedule you for an interview?
- How many different problems will you be able to offer your experience as a solution?

Hopefully you got the point. One STAR story from you will not be applicable to all the different opportunities you will uncover. I recommend you write 20 or more STAR stories. That sounds like a lot of work, doesn't it? Here's a clue on how to make it easier: Start with the STAR story I recommended above. "Tell me about your biggest accomplishment to date." Once you've written that story, consider how you could use that same story to answer the following questions.

1. Tell a story about how you showed leadership.
2. Tell a story about how you developed and implemented a strategy.
3. Tell a story about how you delegated responsibility.
4. Tell a story about how you received/accepted constructive feedback.
5. Tell a story about how you met a tight deadline.
6. Tell a story about how you demonstrated customer service.

Including the original story, you've now created a total of seven STAR stories.

Repeat the process with two more major stories that apply to you but are somewhat unique from each other. From each one, create six more stories as we've done above. Now you have a total of 21 STAR stories to choose from when you eventually are being interviewed and you are looking to tell a story in response to a hiring manager's question.

I recommend you read a paperback book available from Amazon:

"The STAR Interview: How to Tell a Great Story, Nail the Interview and Land Your Dream Job" By Misha Yurchenko and Steve Krumlauf.

In the early parts of this book, you'll learn about how to do the research to write meaningful STAR stories. The latter part of the book tells about how to use STAR stories in an interview.

LinkedIn

A LinkedIn profile provides an additional way for you to tell your story. The LinkedIn profile is uniquely different from your resume. You need both. For the most part, the LinkedIn profile is static whereas your resume will need to be customized for each customer.

<u>Your Profile URL</u>

When you open your LinkedIn account, you'll get an automatically generated URL. I encourage you to change your URL as follows:
- Go to your profile
- At the top right of your profile page click "Edit public profile & URL"
- At the top right of the page click the edit pen image button
- Fill in "First Name" and "Last Name"

<u>Profile Photo</u>

You'll want to include a photo because your LinkedIn page will get far more views if you have a photo with your profile. Here are some tips for your photo:
- Make sure you look neat and clean.
- You don't need to be wearing a suit, but don't be wearing your beat-up jeans.
- You want a friendly look, not real serious, but not silly either.
- A profile picture should accentuate your face.
- Make it a close-up of your face as opposed to a whole-body photo.
- The photo should have been taken recently.
- The photo should be a high-resolution quality color photo.
- Keep in mind that the photo is for a professional platform, so make sure it looks professional.
- The best photo will be a professional headshot.

Write in The First Person

Throughout your LinkedIn profile, write in the first person. This will make you sound personal and sincere.

Headline

Right below your name on your Linkedin profile will be your headline. It's one of the first things a visitor will read. You have 120 characters to work with so use a headline that will catch the visitor's attention.

- The headline needs to be relevant
- Include keywords that can help recruiters find you.
- Instead of using your job title, mention a specialty that shows how you benefit your company or customers. This is not about you. It's got to be about a potential employer or customer.
- An example might be: Marketing Program Manager helping clients build a growing business. Over 120 satisfied clients.

Summary

Recruiters are likely to read your headline and your summary. With that information, they'll decide if you have what they're looking for in relation to an open position they're trying to fill. The LinkedIn Summary provides an opportunity to tell your story.in 2000 characters or less (preferably less than 1000 characters).

The Summary should include the following:
- Your most relevant skills (hard skills and soft skills).
- Your most recent job title.
- Describe your responsibilities and achievements.
- Describe your role in managing people (how many, what were their roles).
- Your budgetary management experience.
- Accomplishments that added valuable results for previous employers (not what you did but what made a difference like increased sales, profits, market penetration, customer satisfaction, etc.).

- Add punch to your accomplishments by including metrics and dates.
- Your years of relevant experience.
- Your passion and how that relates to your chosen career path.
- An example of the role you're looking for.
- Make it between 3 and 5 paragraphs long.
- Use bullet points when relevant

Keywords

Keywords are one factor in catching the attention of recruiters on LinkedIn. Identify the keywords that are most appropriate for your industry, for your market, and for your career.

Find at least five job postings for a position that fits your career needs. Print the job postings and highlight all the hard skills, soft skills, and experience requirements. Treat the most frequently used terms as keywords. Include those keywords in your LinkedIn profile's headline, summary, work experience, and skill section.

Work History

Provide up-to-date work history

- Highlight your experience by including jobs that are relevant to where you want to go with your career.
- Use bullet points to clarify information about the type of business, the number of employees, the products or services provided, your role and your accomplishments. Include metrics if they are available.
- Use action words and incorporate skills to demonstrate the impact you made, changes you enacted, initiatives you led and results you delivered.
- Add media (e.g., photos) to develop an appealing representation of your professional history.

Volunteer Experience

Include volunteer work you've done for non-profit organizations. Leadership roles in organizations outside of your professional experience speak volumes regarding your values and priorities.

Skills and Endorsements
- Include a minimum of 5 skills in your profile.
- Get endorsements for your skills.
- Contact people that you've worked with and ask them to provide a recommendation on your LinkedIn profile.

Licenses and Certifications
Whenever you have certifications that are relevant to your career, include them on your LinkedIn profile.

From within your profile, click on "add profile section" and select "licenses and certifications."

Open to New Opportunities?
LinkedIn lets you declare in your profile that you are open to new opportunities. This helps recruiters know you're open to be approached by them.

Review the result
- Once you've written your profile, read it over and see if it's about you or about what you can do for a prospective employer.
- Read it over again looking for relevance. Is it relevant in representing your career interests and desired roles?

I highly recommend that you have a LinkedIn account. There is a Basic (Free) LinkedIn account and a Premium LinkedIn account. For most of you I recommend you start out with the Basic account. You can always upgrade to a Premium account later if you want to access features in Premium. You can always downgrade later to save money

Why LinkedIn?
LinkedIn is the world's largest professional network on the internet. You can use LinkedIn to find the right job or internship, connect and strengthen professional relationships, research companies and people.

As a college student or experienced professional, it's likely that you are very familiar with social media in all its various forms – Facebook, Twitter, Snapchat, Instagram, and more.

You might be a little less familiar with LinkedIn.

- LinkedIn provides the opportunity to build your professional network - which will have lifelong value.
- Through LinkedIn, you can connect with your classmates, prior colleagues, or employers, and even reach out to potential future employers to maintain and develop business relationships.
- You can follow companies you are interested in to find open positions and you can see what skills their current employees must have to determine if that company is a good fit for you.

So, if you haven't yet created a profile, or haven't recently updated yours, here are a few reasons why you should!

Help Employers Find *YOU*

Research has shown that a large percentage of new hires were not actively looking or applying for jobs. These individuals landed their job through recruiters or were referred by someone within their network, like a friend or family member.

Personal referrals are one of the best ways to land a new job because someone is vouching for you - a huge advantage if the hiring manager trusts that person's opinion.

No matter how large your personal network is, though, there are inevitably many companies you may want to work for where you don't have any personal connections.

Even if you are not actively looking for a job, that doesn't mean that companies and recruiters aren't looking for employees like you.

A survey discovered that "*98.2% of recruiters said they used some sort of social media for recruiting. And 97.3% said they used LinkedIn as a recruiting tool.*"

By maintaining your profile, you make yourself available to all these recruiters who are actively using the platform to find job candidates just like you.

Make Your Social Media Presence More Professional

Another reason to have a LinkedIn profile is to help make your social media presence more professional. When you are applying for a job the recruiter or hiring manager will most likely search your name on Google.

Many employers/recruiters find candidates via LinkedIn.

Questions to Ponder

<u>Before receiving this training, what role did story-telling play in your job search? (Select one)</u>
- ☐ 1. I didn't consider storytelling to be a factor in my job search
- ☐ 2. My resume is my personal story
- ☐ 3. My goal was to start an interview with a personal story of mine
- ☐ 4. I prefer to answer interview questions with a story
- ☐ 5. I prefer to answer interview questions with a story relevant to the employer's needs

<u>Now that you've gone through this material,</u>
How have your thoughts changed regarding storytelling? Are you going to commit to developing your own LinkedIn profile?

Secret #2

Stories Make a Difference

The use of stories in an interview is a powerful technique for making your answers to the interview questions more memorable.

Chapter Summary

Many professional men and women are poor story tellers. There are three important parts about effective story telling:
- Your ability to write good stories
- Your ability to remember good stories
- Your ability to tell good stories

Get some help from a good friend that has strong writing skills and someone that can offer constructive criticism to improve your verbal delivery of your STAR stories and the effort will pay off in the end.

If you want to make a positive impression on a hiring manager or a recruiter and you want to step up to that new career, you need STAR stories and a well-written LinkedIn profile.

If you're going to create a LinkedIn profile, please follow through on that commitment. However, you can continue with this training and develop the LinkedIn profile at the end of the training.

Chapter 5 – Career Consideration

> **ISAIAH 43:18-21** (The Message): *"Forget about what's happened; don't keep going over old history. Be alert, be present. I'm about to do something brand new. It's bursting out! Don't you see it?"*

Chapter 5 (Step Three) addresses:
- People that want to step up to that new career.
- Men and women that wanted a career with a fresh start.
- A career change for men over fifty.
- A career or new job role for women over fifty.
- the need to consider a "career change".

The Bureau of Labor Statistics indicates that the average person has about twelve (12) jobs in a lifetime. Other statistics indicate that a person has about six (6) careers in a lifetime.

But isn't a career a job? What differentiates a career from a job? Is it.......?

Column A		Column B
Salaried	OR	Hourly Wage
Professional	OR	Amateur
Exempt	OR	Non-Exempt
College Diploma	OR	High School Diploma
White Collar	OR	Blue Collar

Dictionary.com defines career as:
- an occupation or profession, especially one requiring special training, followed as one's lifework: *He sought a career as a lawyer.*

- a person's progress or general course of action through life or through a phase of life, as in some profession or undertaking: *His career as a soldier ended with the armistice.*

Dictionary.com defines job as:
- a piece of work, especially a specific task done as part of the routine of one's occupation or for an agreed price: *She gave him the job of mowing the lawn.*

There are other terms that people use that are very similar. But they tend to further confuse the definition. Trying to understand the issue that separates the terms, let's try to simplify it with an article titled The Process of Career Transition. That article written by Kit Harrington Hayes goes on to say:
- When you leave one job and take another doing pretty much the same things in the same industry, you are making a job change.
- When you leave a job for another that involves performing a different function or performing the same function but in a different industry, you are making a career transition.
- Job changes are usually easy and straight forward, with little disruption to the rest of your life.

For this eBook, the target audience is described by the terms in Column A above. This is not a perfect way to describe my target audience as there are people described by Column B that will find this eBook to be very helpful in their search for new employment.

You'll note that the title of this eBook is "Step Up to That New Career". Anybody can read this book and benefit from it if they are seeking a career change, a career transition, or they wanted a new professional job within their existing career.

I respect people that are characterized by Column B. This eBook is not written for their benefit because the job market and the challenges these job searchers face are generally different. And that is not the author's expertise.

Are you considering a career change? I'm not recommending that you pursue a career change. But if you are, here are some questions for you to consider.
- Are you wanting to step up to that new career for the right reason?
- Why is your current career not working?
- What are the long-term opportunities if you make a career change?
- What are the long-term opportunities if you don't make a career change?
- Do you have the right transferrable skills for a career change?
- Who can you trust to provide good advice regarding a career change? What financial resources will you need to change careers?

Transferrable Skills

Transferrable skills are the hard skills or soft skills that you identified in Step One (Chapter 3) that will be useful and of valuable to your next employer in your new career or new job role.
Identification of your transferrable skills is very important in a career change.
- What hard skills will be required?
- What soft skills will be required?
- Which of these skills do you already have?
- What skills do you lack?

Transferrable skills can overcome a lack of experience. You may have all the skills you need to qualify for a career change.

2018 Employment statistics that may be helpful in your consideration
- *51% of employees would quit their job if training was not offered.*

- *If a job lacks growth opportunities and avenues for leadership development, 67% of millennials would leave that position.*
- *Nearly 60% of Americans would take a job they love over a job they hate, even if the preferred position paid half the salary they would earn at the job they dislike.*
- *Nearly half of employees said they've quit a job because of a bad manager, 56% think managers are promoted prematurely, and 60% think managers need training.*
- *13.5% of workers admit that company culture will push them to accept another job offer.*
- *One-third of job seekers would pass up the perfect job if the corporate culture was a bad fit.*
- *Among millennials who worked at 5-7 organizations, 34% didn't trust their direct manager, 31% said their organizations don't set goals, and 46% said their organization thought only about profits.*

Worst Mistakes Career Changers Can Make.

- *Failure to consider their passion and purpose in terms of their career.*
- *Irrational thinking that you can make yourself fit in the wrong environment.*
- *Failure to be self-aware of what drives you to make more of an impact on the organization for whom you are currently employed.*
- *Decide solely on the financial opportunity.*
- *Failure to consider how this career change fits with your longer-term career objectives.*

Set realistic career goals:

- *Clarity – Set goals that are specific. Visualize the outcome.*
- *Realistic – Select challenging/realistic goals*
- *Commitment – Visualize achieving the goal. Commit to it.*
- *Accountable – Recruit mentors and be accountable to them.*
- *Achievable – Set reachable goals and commit to achieving them.*

Career Exploration Resources:

The following resources will be very helpful in your consideration of a career change.
    bls.gov/careeroutlook/
    careeronestop.org
    careertoolkit.com/
    myskillsmyfuture.org
    bls.gov/ooh/
    becomeopedia.com

Questions to Ponder

If you are considering a career change, which of the following statements apply to you? (Select all that apply)

- ☐ 1. I would quit my job if training was not offered.
- ☐ 2. Does your job lack growth opportunity and leadership development?
- ☐ 3. Do you look forward to going to work most every day?
- ☐ 4. Do you feel good about your employer's corporate culture?
- ☐ 5. Do you respect your current manager?
- ☐ 6. Are you seriously considering leaving your existing job?
- ☐ 7. Are you planning to make a career change within the next year?

Secret #3

Job Satisfaction

Americans spend 1/3 of their lives at work. But 80% are dissatisfied with their jobs.

The main reason is a mismatch between what they are good at and what they are currently doing.

Chapter Summary

Many statistics documented in this chapter point to a large percentage of professionals that are unhappy with their job. Regardless of your title and your years of experience you report to somebody in your organization. Even if you are the CEO of a for-profit company, you report to a Board of Directors and shareholders. If you are the President in a non-profit organization, you are being watched by the people that contribute money to your organization.

It appears that many people in supervisory, managerial, or other leadership roles in today's organizations are not paying attention to the needs of the subordinates that report to them.

A high percentage of people that have chosen to step up to that new career are unhappy with the person they report to. Without threatening to quit, talk to your manager or supervisor. Try to come to a mutual understanding that represents a win for you and a win for you manager. If you've done that and your differences are irreconcilable, then a career change may be in order. But before you do that, please re-read this chapter. Therein lies some wisdom that should be heeded.

Chapter 6 – Relationship Building

> **ECCLESIASTES 4:10** (The Living Bible): *"If one falls, the other pulls him up; but if a man falls when he is alone, he's in trouble."*

The internet was birthed in January of 1983. The first online job search was founded in 1994. Jeff Taylor founded The Monster Board to collect and post help wanted ads from newspapers around the country. Prior to 1994, the strategy job searchers used to inform friends, family, and contacts requesting advice was "traditional networking."

Since 1994, online job postings became very popular and eventually that technology matured making it possible to apply for jobs online. Online job boards can be categorized as a "cold call" in that the person receiving your job application doesn't know you and you don't know them.

Chapter 6 (Step Four) will address the importance and benefit of relationships. For most job searchers, without a relationship they are unlikely to land a new career or a new job role.

With that thought in mind, I recommend the following:
- Don't go through the employment search alone.
- Ask for advice from people you know, and they know you.

Later in this ten-step process you'll need to start developing relationships as part of a networking strategy. I recommend that you invest time and energy into relationships with people you know and they know you.

You'll eventually need to develop some relationships into Advocates that will provide employee referrals.

Start by developing a list of hot contacts.

What contacts are the best contacts?
Hot Contacts:

Hot contacts are people you know AND they know you. These are people you can turn to for advice.

Start a list of your contacts and include their phone and email information. Target building a list of at least 50 hot contacts.

Note: The only prerequisite for a hot contact is that you know them, and they know you. This includes:
- People that know nothing about the kind of work you do.
- People that don't have the education you do.
- People that aren't in the same generation as you.

The only thing that is important is that YOU KNOW THEM AND THEY KNOW YOU.

Examples of hot contacts include:
- Friends, relatives, neighbors
- Former colleagues
- From a recent employer
- From a group or organization you're associated with
- From previous employers
- Alumni and other school acquaintances
- College roommates
- College roommate's spouse
- College roommate's relatives
- Friends of your grandparents, parents, sister, brother, cousins, or nephews/nieces
- Your doctor, dentist, landlord, accountant, personal trainer, yoga instructor, contractors, lawyers, suppliers
- Associates from clubs, associations, churches, support groups, etc.

Warm Contacts:

Warm contacts are people referred to you by one of your hot contacts.

Apart from a referral from your hot contact, you didn't know these people. However, they know and respect your hot contact. When your hot contact refers you to a warm contact, the warm contact will welcome an invitation to meet with you.

They'll provide you with quality advice because they respect your hot contact and respect the fact that your hot contact referred you to them.

Cold Contacts:

Cold contacts are people you don't know, or they don't know you.
- To try to connect with them is likely a waste of time.
- Cold calls have no emotional connection with you.
- They have no reason to want to support you by providing you with quality advice.
- It's highly unlikely they'll meet with you.

My best advice is "don't waste your time meeting with cold contacts unless there are extenuating circumstances that indicate this might be a valuable connection. You have many other contacts that will be a better resource.

Importance of hot contacts:
- 70% to 90% of positions are filled via someone who knew someone who knew someone.
- In today's job market, with few exceptions, it's all about who you know.
- Your hot contacts are likely to provide you with quality advice if you'll ask them.

Never ask any contact to help you get a job. But they'll feel good if you honor them by asking for their advice.

Do not let introvertive tendencies or self-imposed embarrassment keep you from letting your hot contacts know that you are unemployed and looking for career advice.

Questions to Ponder

(Select all that apply)

- ☐ 1. I am embarrassed that I am unemployed.
- ☐ 2. I am unlikely to ask people that I know for advice.
- ☐ 3. I could make a list of 50 hot contacts.
- ☐ 4. If a hot contact refers me to somebody I don't know, I will make a connection with that warm contact.
- ☐ 5. I will ask my networking contacts for a 30-minute face-to-face meeting.
- ☐ 6. I intend to ask all my contacts for referrals to at least two other people that might be willing to meet with me for the purpose of giving me advice.
- ☐ 7. I am willing to stay in touch with my hot contacts and warm contacts to let them know how my search is going.

Secret #4

It's About Who You Know

Landing a job in today's job market is all about who you know.

In 2016, 70% of people were hired in an organization where they already had a connection in place.   Source: LinkedIn

Chapter Summary

Relationships are to be developed and maintained throughout your career. Many professionals don't recognize the importance of relationships until they need them and don't have them. But the situation isn't hopeless. In this chapter we defined a relationship simply as someone you know, and they know you. That isn't just relationships that you currently have. That includes people you have known in the past; people that you remember. If you remember them, they likely remember you. A good example is people that worked for the same organization as you. It makes no difference that you knew them 5, 10, 15, or 20 years ago. You knew them. You remember them. And they likely remember you. They may have been in a different department. They may be on a different career path than you. But those very relationships may eventually be the key to your landing new employment. Add their names and contact information to your "hot contact list" now. Never ask them to help you get a job. Always refer to the fact that you are "looking for advice."

Chapter 7- Marketing Plan

> *"When making decisions related to career choices, your starting place is understanding God given design which continues to grow and develop throughout your lifetime. As Elizabeth O'Connor says. "We ask to know the will of God without guessing that His will is written in our very beings."*
>
> *https://www.plough.com/en/topics/community/intentional-community/dialogue-in-christian-community*

Chapter 7 (Step Five) addresses marketing alternatives that you need to know. Step Five is important because it lays the foundation for Step Six which is Marketing Action, the execution of your marketing plan.

To help you understand the job market today, I'm going to introduce you to:

- Elevator pitch
- Recruiters
- Online job applications
- Introduction to Networking
- Business cards

Elevator Pitch

Once you've decided you wanted a career with a fresh start or wanted a new professional job, you'll encounter individuals that could be a valuable career connection. Some of those encounters will be planned, and some unplanned. But in many cases, your opportunity will be limited to less than one minute. We call that an elevator pitch, or elevator speech because the available time on an elevator is roughly 30 to 45 seconds. If you met somebody on an elevator and they asked you about yourself, you need to be prepared to answer them with a short pitch that could open the door to a follow-up meeting.

It's best not to go running to every acquaintance or stranger with the intent to tell your story. It might be tempting, but don't go to that extreme.

The importance of an elevator pitch:

It's effective in demonstrating your professional aptitude, strengths and skills. It's useful in multiple situations which makes it especially valuable. It's particularly helpful in a job search.

You should always have some talking points about yourself prepared (so you're ready to take advantage of unexpected opportunities).

You can use your pitch in an interview situation. Whether it's a phone screen or an in-person interview, you'll be asked to provide a summary of who you are, your background and what you want from your next job.

It's a good tool to use in answering "tell me about yourself."

Both a cover letter and summary statement are intended to tell the reader who you are professionally, what work you are passionate about, and why you are qualified to do it in a way that helps you stand out from other applicants. If you've already crafted an elevator pitch, then this is a great way to repurpose it.

An elevator pitch is also beneficial for networking at an event or during a spontaneous encounter.

Whether you're in line at the grocery store, at a cocktail party or an organized professional gathering, the pitch can quickly help new contacts understand why they should connect with you or consider you when an opportunity arises.

An advantage of using an elevator pitch when speaking about your career or aspirations is that you can show you can take the lead. Instead of waiting on the other party to direct the conversation, and potentially away from what you'd like to discuss, you can assertively explain what you have to offer. In many interactions, such as a job interview or mentorship proposition, this can be impressive to your audience—they will be pleased to see you know both what you want and how to ask for it.

How to write and deliver an elevator pitch:

Start by introducing yourself. As you approach someone to pitch to at an event, interview or anything in between, start with an introduction.

- Start your pitch by giving your full name, smile, extend your hand for a handshake and add a pleasantry like, "It's nice to meet you!"
- Summarize what you do.
- Give a summary of your background.
- Include the most relevant information such as your education, work experience and/or any key specialties or strengths.
- If you're not sure what to include, try writing everything that comes to mind down on a piece of paper.
- Once you've recorded it, go through and remove anything that's not absolutely critical to explaining your background and why you've got what your audience may be looking for (you might consider the most important highlights on your resume).
- Once you've got it down to a few points, organize them in a way that makes sense in your story.

Here's an example:

"Hi, my name is Sara. It's so nice to meet you! I'm a PR manager with a special focus in overseeing successful initiative launches from beginning to end. Along with my seven years of professional experience, I recently graduated with my MBA from XYZ University, with a focus on consumer trust and retention..."

Explain what you want

This step will depend on how you're using the pitch.

The "ask" of your pitch could be a consideration for a job opportunity, internship or simply to get contact information.

This is a good opportunity to explain the value you'll bring, why you're a good fit for a job, or generally what your audience might gain from your interaction.

Focus on what you have to offer during this section of the speech.

Let's go back to Sara's pitch:

"Hi, my name is Sara. It's so nice to meet you! I'm a PR manager, specializing in overseeing successful initiative launches from beginning to end. Along with my seven years of professional experience, I recently received my MBA with a focus on consumer trust and retention. I find the work your PR team does to be innovating and refreshing—I'd love the opportunity to put my expertise to work for your company..."

Finish with a call to action

You should end your elevator pitch by asking for or stating what you want to happen next.

If you feel an elevator pitch is appropriate for a certain situation, begin with the goal of gaining new insight or determining next steps.

Examples can include asking for a meeting, expressing interest in a job, confirming you've fully answered an interview question or asking someone to be your mentor.

Asking for what you want can be intimidating, but it's important you give the conversation an action item instead of letting it come to a dead end.

Remember: You've just met this person, so make the ask simple with little required on their part. Here's an example from the pitch we've been building:

"Hi, my name is Sara. It's so nice to meet you! I'm a PR manager, specializing in overseeing successful initiative launches from beginning to end. Along with my 7 years of professional experience, I recently received my MBA with a focus on consumer trust and retention. I find the work your PR team does to be innovating and refreshing—I'd love the opportunity to put my expertise to work for your company. Would you mind if I set up a quick call next week for us to talk about any upcoming opportunities on your team?"

If they agree to your request, be sure to thank them for their time and get their contact information.

End the conversation with a concise and action-oriented farewell, such as, "Thank you for your time, I'll send you a follow-up email tonight. Have a great day!".

If they don't agree to your request, gracefully end the conversation with a polite, "I understand, thank you for your time! If it's all right, I'll send you a follow-up email and see if there's a better time for us to connect."

Recruiters

Recruiters are hired by employers to staff specific positions. They aren't like real estate agents with multiple listings.

What do you get out of working with recruiters?
The best part of working with a third-party recruiter is that you both have the same goal: finding you a job with a great employer that fits your skills, culture, and background.
A good recruiter can help you:
Keep your search confidential instead of sending your resume out into the void
Recruiters are a direct conduit to the employer for your application, complete with recommendation and references
They can tell you about unposted opportunities.
- *A recruiter can provide insight into where you stand compared to other candidates interviewing for a position*

- *They can differentiate opportunities (and give you the unposted details on a role).*
- *They can offer nuanced, current market insights on things like salary ranges for different roles.*
- *They can provide you with honest feedback on your expectations.*
- *They can help you by reviewing resumes, preparing for interviews, and offering salary and benefits negotiation advice.*
- *They can give ongoing job advice and support – many recruiters have worked with the same candidates for years and have them in mind when the perfect opportunity opens.*
- *If you meet with a recruiter and they tell you they aren't the best resource for what you're looking for right now, they'll also give you feedback!*

What you need to know about recruiters

Here are some facts to help you understand a recruiter's mindset:

- They must meet their client expectations first and foremost. They can advocate for you but are not only representing you.
- Recruiters are not career coaches.
- Working with a recruiter should always be free for the candidate, but keep in mind that the employer is paying the bill. If you want a career coach, there are some amazing coaches who have the tools and training to be a huge benefit to your search. As expected, these personalized coaching services do come at a cost to you.
- Although they might like you and advocate for you, recruiters are also not decision makers on who to move forward in the interview process. They usually pass on the good or bad news.
- It's not personal when they tell you they can't be a good resource. They don't want to waste your time or set false expectations. Since the recruiter is tasked with delivering 110% of the client's expectations on any job placement, candidates should expect to be moved forward or selected only when they are truly the most competitive candidate for the position.
- Recruiters are typically working on a limited number of positions at any given time. That means, if you are a Marketing Coordinator and they aren't working on a Marketing Coordinator role, it could be a while before you hear from them. It doesn't mean you aren't a good candidate! It simply means that they are working strategically on other positions at the time.
- Recruiters also focus their energy on the roles they are most likely to fill quickly, and typically won't check back with candidates who aren't a fit for their current roles, just to say they don't have anything for you. They are, however, happy to hear from you and provide an update when you have questions.

Should I work with a recruiter?

Working with a recruiter can be a great resource in your search. But to make sure you're not wasting your time; you should do your homework on the agency and recruiter you're considering.

Most recruiters specialize across geographical locations, job titles, and industries. Look for those organizations who work with companies that appeal to you. Look at their track record.

Speak with trusted friends and other connections about their experiences with staffing firms.

Keep in mind that reviews typically span both ends of the spectrum. They either loved the agency or a specific recruiter because they got a great job, or they were upset by a poor experience (and/or they had unrealistic expectations).

In general, because of the fees that go into using their service, recruiters are expected to identify job candidates who check every box the client is looking for. So, recruiters are great for folks on a clear career path, with experience in the field they're pursuing.

However, they are usually unable to "take a chance" on someone with a nontraditional background for the role they are recruiting for because most clients expect to see the type of professional they asked for in the job description.

Types of recruiters:

- Outplacement recruiter - Often an employer will hire an outplacement company to help recently downsized workers. Outplacement services provide resume and interviewing assistance, career counseling, etc.
- Corporate recruiter - A corporate recruiter is the most common type. Companies often use contractors to work as recruiters to avoid outside agency fees. They are paid a salary.
- Contingency recruiter - Contingency recruiters do a full-time employee search on a contingency basis. They are paid only if the candidate is hired. The company pays a flat fee or a percentage of the first year's salary once they've hired the recruiter's candidate. Job hunters do not have to pay a fee.

- Retained recruiter - The employer pays the retained recruiter a retainer fee. This initial fee is usually a fixed amount paid upfront and it is paid irrespective of whether the placement was completed. The remaining fee is paid upon a successful hire. Retained recruiters are typically focused on recruiting candidates for high level positions in the employer's firm.

How to attract a recruiter

Recruiters will be interested in you if you have a marketable background.

You're more likely to attract a recruiter if you:

- Develop a LinkedIn profile with endorsements, recommendations, work samples, etc.
- Place a strong resume on job search engine sites like Indeed, Monster, and niche sites in your field.
- Develop a reputation in a professional association.
- Make a presentation at a conference.
- Hold an office in an association.
- Publish an article, report, or book.

Online Job Applications

Online job applications became a popular job search marketing strategy primarily because it was much easier to apply for a job online.

Once you've found a job posted online that looks attractive, you can fill out the online in a matter of minutes, attach a resume, attach a cover letter, and send the application from the comfort of your own home or office.

Prior to the advent of online job postings, most hiring was local because jobs were posted in the want ads of a local newspaper or people learned about the opening through word-of-mouth communication.

Job Search Engines versus Job Boards:
Job boards are typically more focused on a particular industry, location or job type (e.g., freelance, contract, remote), while job search engines like Indeed aggregate a wide range of job listings from thousands of online sources. That's why job search engines are also known as job aggregators.

10 Best Job Search Websites of 2021:
Indeed   Best overall
Monster   Runner-up, best overall
Glassdoor Best for employer research
FlexJobs   Best for remote jobs
Ladders   Best for experienced managers
AngelList Best for startup jobs
LinkedIn   Best for connecting with recruiters
Getwork   Best for up-to-date listings
Scouted   Best for recent college graduates
Snagajob   Best for hourly workers

Online Application Statistics:

Once a job hunter identifies a job posting that is worthy of their online application, they can apply online.

- An average of 250 applications are received for every job posting.
- Approximately 75% of the resumes will be disqualified and rejected by an Applicant Tracking System (ATS).
- An application that is disqualified/rejected is not forwarded to the employer that posted the job.
- 4 to 6 of the applicants that made it through the ATS will be invited for an interview.
- 1 to 3 will be invited back for a final interview.
- 1 will be offered the job.
- 20% of the time, the applicant that received the offer will reject it. Generally, jobs are rejected because the candidate that received the offer was not satisfied with the terms of the offer, or they had another offer that they chose to accept.

Unfortunately, jobs that are posted online represent the minority of job openings. In other words, employers do not post most job openings.

Unadvertised jobs:

Approximately 60% to 80% of jobs are not advertised. In other words, most job openings are hidden from the public's view via online job postings.

The best access to unadvertised jobs is through networking.

Introduction to Networking

Networking is the action or process of interacting with others to exchange information, develop professional relationships, and promote social relationships.

Networking can be helpful for:
- Learning about industries you might want to consider.
- Learning about market trends that might influence your career choice.
- Learning about new technologies that might impact your list of potential employers.
- Learning about alternative career choices.

In this eBook, networking is about interacting with individuals from whom you can gain information and advice that will help you in the pursuit of your chosen career.

We'll go into much more detail on networking strategies in Step 6

Business Cards

A common fault of job searchers is that they wait too long to order business cards. It's never too early for you to purchase business cards. Get them now and begin carrying them with you wherever you go.

When you have a face-to-face encounter with a person that asks you what you do, tell your story and exchange business cards. Failing to do so may turn out to be a lost opportunity.

When you communicate with an individual or a group via video conference (e.g., Zoom), ask for their contact information and provide your contact information. Get clarification on spelling.

What to include on a business card

In most cases, you don't need to spend a lot of money on your business cards. You can get a local printer to print some for you, or you can order business cards online.

The basic information to include on your business card should be:
- Your full name
- Your email address
- Your cell phone number
- Your LinkedIn profile URL (if you have one)

Initially, you don't need:
- Color
- Photos
- Graphics
- Two-sided printing

Questions to Ponder

(Select all that apply)

- ☐ 1. I have written an Elevator Pitch in the past
- ☐ 2. I expect to use an Elevator Pitch with future contacts
- ☐ 3. I have worked with a Recruiter in the past
- ☐ 4. I would be interested in working with a Recruiter in the future
- ☐ 5. Based on what you read in Step #5; I am inclined to continue to apply for jobs online in response to an online job posting
- ☐ 6. I have never been offered a job in response to an online job application in the past?
- ☐ 7. I was surprised to learn that most jobs are not posted online

Secret #5

Unposted Job Openings

60% to 80% of job openings are not posted online which means they aren't filled through online job applications.

Chapter Summary

Elevator pitches, recruiters, online applications, networking, and the use of business cards, are the basics when it comes to establishing a marketing plan..

In terms of what you should do now, I suggest you proceed as follows:

1. Write your elevator pitch
2. Practice delivering your elevator pitch so you can communicate it smoothly when an opportunity presents itself.
3. Order 150 business cards. No graphics, no photo, no need for double sided. Carry them with you and pass them out to anybody that shows an interest in you as a potential candidate for a job opening.
4. Develop your LinkedIn profile in hopes that it will attract recruiters that may have an employment opportunity they are trying to fill for one of their clients.
5. Proceed to Chapter 8 (Step Six) where you'll learn about the use of networking in your Marketing Action.

Chapter 8 – Marketing Action (Networking)

> **ISAIAH 40:28-31 (NLT):** *"Have you never understood? The Lord is the everlasting God, the Creator of all the earth. He never grows weak or weary. No one can measure the depths of his understanding. He gives power to the weak and strength to the powerless. Even youths will become weak and tired and young men will fall in exhaustion. But those who trust in the Lord will find new strength. They will soar on high on wings like eagles. They will run and not grow weary. They will walk and not faint."*

Chapter 8 (Step Six) will cover specific actions you can take to market yourself. The focus will be on the use of networking. Networking strategies provide the greatest potential for an interview. In this chapter we'll include:

- The Gated Market
- Informational Interviews
- Professional Association Groups
- Strategic Use of the LinkedIn Network
- Targeted Networking
- How to prepare for and conduct networking meetings.

The Gated Market

In the real estate market, there are housing developments that are surrounded by a wall. Gated communities don't accept visitors unless the visitor is given access by someone authorized within the community. So, to summarize, entrance is made through gates that:
- Can be opened with the use of a code
- Can be opened with a wireless transmitted code
- Can be opened by a guard at the gate
- Can be opened by an authorized person inside the community

In the job market, many businesses operate like gated communities. To gain access to Human Resources or a Hiring Manager you need somebody on the inside to let you in.

Most jobs within the business community are found via a referral from somebody on the inside of the business.

According to a 2021 report, *70% of people found jobs through personal connections inside the business. That same report indicated that 85% of positions were filled via networking.*

Earlier in this training, networking was defined as the action or process of interacting with others to exchange information, develop professional relationships, and promote social relationships

In job search, networking is about asking for advice when interacting with individuals to gain information that will help in your job hunting.

In this training we'll take a close look at Informational Interviewing as an example of a networking strategy.

Informational Interview

We're going to look at a real-life example of an informational interview. Note: It's called an information interview but it's not an interview with a Hiring Manager. Pay close attention to each step in the process and how it contributed to the results. The name of the person will not be used. Instead, I'll refer to the job searcher as Mary.

- Mary was looking for a career in the healthcare industry.
- She recognized there would be strong competition if she applied for an advertised job in her preferred role. Her odds of getting such a position were poor.
- She decided her chances of getting a job would be better if she used a networking strategy.
- To improve her credibility in her search for a job, and to improve her readiness for such a career, she attended relevant classes.
- Mary searched LinkedIn for a person currently in a role like the job Mary wanted. She found a person she could message within LinkedIn.
- Mary sent that LinkedIn member a message pointing out their common interest (which was their chosen career). In that message Mary mentioned her interest in a full-time job in a role like the one her contact was in. And Mary asked to chat.
- Mary's contact responded the next day and welcomed the opportunity to chat and was willing to answer Mary's questions.
- They met – In their meeting Mary's contact asked Mary many questions to learn more about Mary's background.
- Eventually Mary's contact said that Mary would be perfect for a role identical to hers.
- Mary's contact offered to look within her company for any postings she might not be aware of, and she promised to refer Mary to the Hiring Manager when the right position was posted.

- Four days later Mary saw a job posted in her contact's organization and Mary applied for that job.
- Mary notified her contact of the open position and her contact talked to the hiring manager on Mary's behalf.
- The following week, Mary was hired.

This is not an unusual situation. It happens often. All it takes is a person like Mary that will take the initiative to make it happen.

The information interview, if conducted in a professional manner, with preparation and excellent questions, could convince the influential person (in the example that was Mary's contact) to open doors for you.

At the end of the interview, always ask for referrals to other people you should meet with.

Don't ask your contact to help you get a job and don't expect to end up with a job, at least not right away.

Ask them for permission to follow-up with an additional question in the future.

Thank them and confirm the spelling of their name, their title, and their email address.

If you're planning to adopt the informational interview strategy, consider these questions to ask when you start to converse with your contact?
- My understanding is that your role is _____.
- What do you like most about your role?
- What career path did you take to get that role?
- What are your biggest challenges in that role?
- What advice would you give me if I wanted to be in a similar position in the future?

Note: If you're doing all the talking, it isn't an informational interview. Focus on getting information from your contact.

Professional Associations

As a professional, you are encouraged to join a professional association. Get involved, Get known. Once you're recognized as a contributor to the association, you'll be able to network with leaders in the association asking for their advice for advancing your career.

Click here for a directory of professional associations.

LinkedIn Groups / Facebook Groups

There are many LinkedIn groups. In the LinkedIn Search Bar, type in the word group. Look at the opportunities. Join the appropriate group. Get involved. Contribute some of your experience to other group members. When you become known, you'll be able to network with others in the group asking for their advice for advancing your career.

>Note: There are similar groups in Facebook. Follow the above action within a Facebook Group.

Targeted Networking

(Note: This is not the same as traditional networking)
- Contact members in your hot contact list. Ask for potential employers they recommend.
- Build your potential employer list until you've got roughly 30 potential employers on your list. if you need more potential employers to add to your list do additional research in business journals and LinkedIn
- Research each of your potential employers. Narrow down the list based on your preferences.
- End up with roughly 15 employers that now become your target.
- Make connection with at least one employee in each of your target employers. Learn about the company culture and the problems the company needs to solve.
- Based on your networking meeting, customize your resume.
- Send your customized resume to your networking contact.
- Maintain and strengthen your relationship with networking contacts.
- Encourage selected networking contacts to become an Advocate for you within their organization.

Networking Meetings

Preparation for a networking meeting

Preparation is the key whether the networking meeting is face-to-face or a virtual meeting.
- Ask for a 30-minute meeting.
- Avoid telephone networking meetings.
- Do not provide your contact with your resume prior to this meeting.
- Prepare a list of question you want to ask

How to conduct a networking meeting

Note: Networking is a means of relating to another person for the purpose of gathering information and getting advice. The goal of the meeting should not be to get a job.
- Start by demonstrating a positive attitude and positive energy.
- If by chance you identify a common interest the two of you have, make note of that for future communication.
- Exchange business cards at the start of the meeting. Be a good listener.
- Ask open-ended questions that keep the other person talking in hopes they will reveal opportunities and needs that are relevant to you and to their employer.
- Show interest in your contact's career. How did they get their job? What do they like about their employer? Why do they like to work there? What are the contact's longer-term goals?

If the person is a busy professional that you haven't gotten to know well, get to the point so they don't resent you wasting their time.

In this case,
- Be specific in your request.
- Articulate what you're looking for.
    a. Is it a reference?
    b. Is it an insider's take on the industry?
    c. Is it a referral?

      d. Do you want them to make an introduction to someone else?

What are some general subjects to discuss in a networking meeting?

To get the best results from a networking meeting, it's critical that you, the Job Hunter, ask open-ended questions that will get your networking contact talking about subjects that will help you determine three things, namely,

1. What is your contact's perspective on his/her career that brought them to their current position and their satisfaction regarding the role they're currently in?
2. What is your contact's perspective on their employer's industry and market?
3. What are the challenges their employer has faced in the past and is currently experiencing now?

Networking meeting questions to ask:

Reminder: Networking is a means of relating to another person for the purpose of gathering information and getting advice. The goal of the meeting should not be to get a job.

- How has the industry changed in the past 5 years?
- What have been some recent changes in the company?
- How has your career changed recently?
- Have the company's customer's expectations changed?
- Has the customer base grown, stayed level, or declined recently?
- Has the morale of the employees changed? If so, how?

Ask questions that will reveal whether an employment opportunity is a good fit for you.

At the end of the meeting ask for referrals to 2 or more new contacts.

Networking meeting follow-up:

After the meeting, if your networking meeting caused you to want to consider any upcoming job opportunities at that company, customize your resume based on what you learned at the meeting.

Send your contact a thank you email

- If your contact requested a copy of your resume, send them your customized resume along with the thank you email.
- Communication – Send a thank you email within 48 hours of your meeting.
- Gratitude – Express appreciation for the time taken and for the valuable information your contact provided.
- Action Items – Document any follow-up action items agreed to at the meeting.
- Respond – Attach any papers, articles, or resume you agreed to send.
- Assistance – Offer your assistance to your networking contact. Small kindnesses open doors.
- Reflection – If you connected on any other area of interest (e.g., a favorite sport, a book you're currently reading, a vacation you recently took, family activities, college experience, etc.) continue a dialog on that subject of common interest.

Turn the networking connection into a relationship

Don't be a hit-and-run networker: getting what you want and running.

- Nurture the relationship.
- Help them to get to know you
- Get to know them as well.
- Once the relationship has developed ask them to be an advocate for you.
- If they say no, ask what it would take for them to be willing to be an advocate for you. Then pursue that goal.
- If they say yes, ask them to investigate existing or upcoming open positions that might be of interest to you.
- Send them the latest copy of your customized resume for them to forward to decision makers in their company or to a hiring manager that has posted a new open position that may be of interest to you.

Secret #6

The Importance of Networking

More than 85% of respondents to a LinkedIn survey indicated that networking was the most effective way to get a job.

Source: LinkedIn

Questions to Ponder
(Select all that apply)

☐ 1. I have experienced the "gated market" where I couldn't make connection with decision makers inside a business.

☐ 2. I know the kind of position or role I would like to be in.

☐ 3. I can do the research to identify somebody to connect with for the purpose of getting advice regarding my career.

☐ 4. I have networked with people in the past for the purpose of getting advice.

☐ 5. The information in Step #6 will be helpful in preparing me for a networking meeting.

☐ 6. I recognize the importance of submitting a customized resume to a networking contact after I have had a meeting with that contact.

☐ 7. I have never developed a relationship to the point where I could ask that person to be an advocate for me, but I'm willing to do it.

Chapter Summary

In this chapter I've introduced you to five job search networking strategies. They are all powerful strategies. I hope you paid attention to the following:

According to a 2021 report, *70% of people found jobs through personal connections inside the business.*
That same report indicated that *85% of positions were filled via networking.*
I've also introduced you to the concept of the "Gated Network". It is an accurate description of today's job market. Without an Advocate that is on the inside of the gate, you'll find it very difficult to get consideration from an employer that does not advertise their jobs online.

I've given you considerable information that will help you with the networking process. Take advantage of this information. It will make a difference for you in your search for that next employment.

Chapter 9 – Resume Customization

> **PROVERBS 12:17** (The Message): *"Truthful witness by a good person clears the air, ... but liars lay down a smoke screen of deceit."*

The general belief in the job market is that a well written resume will yield job interviews. There are exceptions but, without a doubt, a poorly written resume is a turn-off to hiring managers.

Chapter 9 (Step Seven) you're going to learn how to write a resume that will capture the attention of hiring managers.

There are many HR personnel, trainers, coaches, and online resources that will advise you on how to write a resume. I've been teaching professionals for years in how to write a resume. My method works.

I'm going to provide you with information as follows:
- What is a resume?
- Resume Table of Contents
- Resume Sweet Spot
- Remainder of Resume Content
- Formatting a Resume
- Customizing Your Resume

What Is a Resume?

A resume is an advertisement for the purpose of landing an interview for a job you desire.

In most cases, the Hiring Manager doesn't care about the good work you've done.

Focus on the problem(s) the Hiring Manager is trying to solve. Communicate the value you bring that can contribute to solving their problem(s). How would you know what their problems are that need to be solved? You need to:
- Do research on the company
- Read recent news articles on the company
- Study their website
- Conduct networking meetings with current and past employees of the company (but not the Hiring Manager). Ask for advice, not a job.

A Hiring Manager will be most interested in your past manager's perspective on how you impacted the past manager's business. This message must be conveyed in your resume.

Resume Table of Contents

- The Sweet Spot
- Heading
- Summary
- Key Accomplishments
- Core Competencies
- Remainder of the Resume
- Professional Experience
- Education
- Professional Organizations
- Volunteer Activity/Awards

What is the Sweet Spot?

The sweet spot is the top half of the first page of the resume. If your resume doesn't capture the attention and interest of a Hiring Manager after reading the top half of the first page, they're unlikely to read the remainder. So, let's look at what needs to be communicated in the "sweet spot".

Resume Sweet Spot Template

The Heading:
Your name (first, last) on the top line.
Contact information:
- You cell phone number
- Your email address
- Your LinkedIn Profile URL

Do not include:
- Home telephone number (unless you don't have a cell phone)
- Your street address, city, state, and zip code

Your desired job title
- If you are applying for a job where they are using a different title on their job description or online job posting, change your title to match the title the potential employer is using.

Key Skills:
- Right under the job title, include three key skills.
- Pick three skills that appear to be emphasized in the employer's job description, skills you legitimately can claim as your skills.

- Format the listing of the three skills as follows:
  SKILL #1 | SKILL #2 | SKILL #3
  Notice the vertical bar (aka PIPE) separating the three skills. This is required. Each skill should be a one or two-word skill name.

Summary Statement:
- The heading should read one of the following:
  a. Summary Statement, or
  b. Professional Summary
- Don't use bullet points. But the following bullet points include the content of the narrative summary statement.
  a. Start with 2 or 3 highly relevant action words from the job posting.
  b. Reference your years of experience and how that is relevant to your ability to solve the employer's problem.
  c. Identify one major accomplishment and 2 or 3 areas of excellence that make you unique.
- Example of a summary statement
  Reliable organized leader with over 5 years of excellence in reducing labor cost and improving time-to-market. Led a cross functional team in improving gross margin by 4% on a major product line in 2020. Expert in continuous improvement, team building, and customer service.

Accomplishments:
- Include at least three or four bullet point STAR stories that describe a situation, task, action, and result that contributed to the growth or a previous employer.
- Make sure the items you list directly relate to the position you are applying for. Start each point with an action word.

Core Competencies:
- Put together a list a list of keywords that represent your areas of excellence. Ideally it should include:
- 1 to 3 hard skills (if the job requires hard skills)
- 3 to 4 soft skills
- 1 or 2 CliftonStrengths
- 2 or 3 Unique Talents
- Chain all of them together (with vertical bar separators as described in Key Skills above) in 3 or lines of text with the title Core Competencies.

This is the end of the "Sweet Spot" in your resume.

Professional Experience (aka Work History)
1. Start with the company name for your most recent employer.
2. On the same line (to the right) list the start date and end date for that employment.
3. On the second line, include your title followed on the same line with the city and state where you were employed in this position.
4. On the following lines use bullet points that describe the nature of the employer's business and your main responsibility. Make sure the information is written to be meaningful to a potential employer. List your most important accomplishments and responsibilities that are relevant to a potential employer. Use metrics whenever possible without disclosing confidential information.
- Repeat steps 1 through 4 above for each subsequent employment or role that you held.

- Note: Only provide dates for employment held within the past 10 to 15 years.

Education:
- List all post high school education including the name of the school and the city and state where that education took place.
- The dates of that education are not required.
- List the degree or certificate you earned, and the field of study associated with that degree or certificate.
- If you are in the process of getting that degree or certificate, state that and the target completion date.

Ongoing Professional Development:
- List other education or training you received in support of your career. That includes:
    a. Continuing education classes
    b. Online training
    c. Certifications received
    d. Relevant seminars

Volunteer Activity and Recognition Awards
- Identify volunteer activity, professional associations you've been involved with, and any awards you've received.
- This information speaks to your character. The activities do not need to line up with your career.

Do Not Include:
- Your resume should not state "References Available Upon Request"
- If you have gaps in your resume, you do not need to explain them in the resume. But you do need to be prepared in an interview to speak to the nature of the gap and what you did during that gap.

Resume Tips for Men & Women Over 50

If you are looking for a career change for men over fifty, career change for women over fifty, or a new job role for women over fifty, it will be helpful if you pay attention to the following resume tips.
1. Dates: Do not include dates on your education. Include dates on Professional Experience within the most recent 10 years.
2. You don't need to meet 100% of the requirements in a job posting. 60% or more is acceptable.
3. Ongoing Professional Development section: List classes, seminars, and certifications. you've received since you entered the job market. You're still interested in learning new things.
4. Don't provide too much information, especially clues that might hint at your age (e.g., dated words, old email services). Too much content is an indication of age.
5. Exclude employment history that is old and irrelevant.
6. Limit the length of your resume to 2 pages.
7. Professional experience more than 15 years old does not need to be on the resume. Include it only if it's relevant to the position you are applying for.

Recommended Resume Format

Font Size	10 to 12 point
Font Style	Easily read – no script fonts
Heading Format	Consistent
Bullet Points	In Professional Experience only
Page Margins	0.75 inches minimum
Use of Columns	1 column, left justified, no tables
Photos or Graphics	Do not use
Page Length	2 pages filled in

Applicant Tracking Systems

Many companies rely on 3rd party Applicant Tracking Systems (ATS) to assist with the electronic screening of employment applications.

The intent is to eliminate unqualified candidates when the requirements stated in the employer's job posting (e.g., skills) don't match the content in the candidate's resume.

75% of online applications are rejected by the ATS and they never get to the employer.

JobScan is a tool that gives job hunters an instant analysis of how well their resume is tailored for a particular job.

Just visit JobScan and paste in the resume text and the text of the job posting (no PDF formatted documents are accepted).

JobScan will compare the two documents to look for missing skills in the resume. If you don't believe you exhibit a specific skill, don't include it in your resume.

Customize Your Resume

Every resume that is going to be submitted with a job application should be customized.

Obtain the job description or job posting for the job
- Identify the required skills, experience, and education specified in the job description or job posting.
- Demonstrate how you are the right person for this employer's job (be specific).
- Consider your fit in terms of soft skills and personality.
- Customize your resume for that employer.
- Consider this article to answer this question about your resume: "Why your resume will be overlooked even though you are completely qualified?"
- Customize the resume before every application.

Questions to Ponder

<u>(Select all that apply)</u>
- ☐ 1. I like the tip to use JobScan.com.
- ☐ 2. I haven't used customized resumes in the past.
- ☐ 3. I plan to customize all my resumes in the future.

Secret #7

The Importance of Metrics

When you have metrics to back up your claims in your resume, and you add action verbs to your resume, then what you are stating is more believable doubling your chance of getting invited for an interview.

Secret #8

Customized Resume

The majority of hiring managers consider a customized resume the number one tactic for applicants trying to boost their chance of getting hired.

All resumes should be customized.

Chapter Summary

At the beginning of this chapter, I pointed out that "The general belief in the job market is that a well written resume will yield job interviews. There are exceptions but, without a doubt, a poorly written resume is a turn-off to hiring managers." I would like to point out that the Steps 1 through 6 of this eBook will help you to write a better resume. That is to say that skipping Steps 1 through 6 of eBook will not produce the quality of resume that could have been produced had they given serious consideration to the training they skipped.

I have personally coached many professionals. After looking at many resumes, I've discovered they were not of the quality that will result in an invitation to an interview.

I must also emphasize that all resumes must be customized. Your resume must connect with the needs of the hiring organization. Organizations are not clones of each other. They all have their unique set of problems. Unless your resume provides evidence that you understand their problem, and you are equipped to solve their problem, you are unlikely to be interviewed.

Chapter 10 – Cover Letter Writing

> **PSALM 145:6** (NLT): *"Your awe-inspiring deeds will be on every tongue; I will proclaim your greatness."*

In Chapter 8 (Step 8) we'll address the following:
- Purpose of the cover letter
- The pros and cons of a cover letter
- Cover letter header and salutation
- Cover letter body

The cover letter purpose is to:
- Emphasize those skills, education, and/or experience that makes you qualified for the position you are applying for.
- Demonstrate your written communication skills.
- Help differentiate you from your competition.
- Identify the employee that referred you to the job.

Pros and Cons

If an employee referred you for this job, attach a cover letter and reference the name of the employee that referred you and the position you are applying for
- If the employer requires it, send a cover letter.
- If a cover letter is not required, and you are weak in your written communication skills, you may be better off not submitting one.
- Better, yet, find somebody that is a good writer that can help you write your cover letter.

Cover Letter Header and Salutation

Include your name, email address, and cell phone number on the cover letter. Use the same info as your resume.

Address your cover letter to the Hiring Manager using their name. If you don't know it, get it.

- If you don't know their name, call or email the company and ask for the correct spelling for the Hiring Manager's name as a way to get their name.
- If you are unable to get the Hiring Manager's name, consider replacing it with their job title, team, or department.

Reference the exact title of the position you are applying for, on a separate line, or in your opening sentence.

Cover Letter Body

- Start with a strong opening stating the position you're applying for and show passion for the position and the company.
- Mention why you want to work there and what makes this opportunity unique.
- Describe your skills and expertise and how they are a perfect match for the position or organization.
- Present your most relevant qualifications and accomplishments in detail.
- Incorporate job posting keywords and phrases into your cover letter.
- Include examples of how your skills have been effective for previous employers.
- Include a STAR story about how you stand out from other candidates as the best person for the position.

Conclusion

Include a call to action such as a referral to information in your resume, an invitation for an interview, or a time that would work well for you to talk.
End with:
Warm Regards
Your first and last name

Questions to Ponder

(Select all that apply)
- ☐ 1. I have never written a cover letter.
- ☐ 2. I always write my own cover letter.
- ☐ 3. I take pride in the cover letters I've written.

Secret #9

The Importance of Cover Letters

Roughly 46% of Hiring Managers require a cover letter. It's a great way to express your interest in the organization and a way to stand out above other candidates.

Chapter Summary

Historically, all employers required submission of a cover letter along with the resume. When submitted in an online application, it used to be that the application wouldn't let you submit the application if you didn't attach the cover letter. That has changed. Some employers do not require a cover letter. Not all online applications prohibit submitting the application if there is no cover letter attached.

On the other hand, I recommend you submit a cover letter with each application whether it is submitted in person, by mail, or in an online application.

As I stated earlier, the purpose for the cover letter is to:
- Emphasize those skills, education, and/or experience that makes you qualified for the position you are applying for.
- Demonstrate written communication skills.
- Help differentiate you from your competition.
- Identify the employee that referred you.

If you submit a well-written cover letter, it may help to differentiate you from others competing for the same job. It may make a difference in your being invited for an interview.

Chapter 11 – Management Interviewing

> **PHILIPPIANS 4:6-7 (NLT):** *"Don't worry about anything; instead, pray about everything. Tell God what you need, and thank him for all he has done. Then you will experience God's peace, which exceeds anything we can understand. His peace will guard your hearts and minds as you live in Christ Jesus."*

The key to your success in an interview has to do with how well you prepare for an interview. This lesson is going to cover:
- Face-to-Face interviews
- Virtual interviews
- Telephone interviews
- Executive Interviews

Face-to-Face Interview

The thought of having to be at the center of attention in an interview can bring on a high level of anxiety for most anybody.

Anxiety can be an interview killer.

Now you're going into an interview hoping it will result in an employment offer.

It's common for you to be nervous, worried, or anxious.

What can you do to keep those emotions from hurting your interview performance?

The answer lies in preparation. Follow this training to ensure that you are prepared.

When asked a question: take your time to gather your thoughts before you answer the question.

Research the organization
Be able to demonstrate that you've researched the organization.
- The company's goals
- Past business results
- Recent news sources
- The culture and environment of this business

For more information on researching a company, go to:
https://www.indeed.com/career-advice/finding-a-job/the-complete-guide-to-researching-a-company

Common questions you may be asked
- Tell me about yourself
- What are your strengths?
- Tell me about your weaknesses?
- Why do you want to work here?
- Why did you leave your last job?
- Why should we choose you?
- What motivates you?

For more of these questions and how to answer them, go to:
Your Ultimate Guide to Answering the Most Common Interview Questions:

Behavioral Interview Questions

Recent hiring practices make more use of behavioral interviewing questions asking the candidate to share their thoughts on how they would respond to specific situations.

One of the best ways to answer behavioral questions is by using the STAR Interview Technique.

Behavioral questions are answered by describing a situation you handled in the past and what you would do if you faced a similar situation in the future.

How to break your response into parts to provide a better response:

- Situation –
    a. Think of a situation like what the interviewer is asking you about that had a successful outcome.
    b. It doesn't have to be work related if its relevant.
- Task -
    a. Describe your responsibility in this situation. Keep it specific but concise.
    b. Make sure you highlight specific challenges you faced.
- Action
    a. Describe exactly what you did.
    b. How did you complete the task you were assigned?
    c. Highlight traits (qualities) that a hiring manager will find desirable (e.g., initiative, teamwork, leadership, dedication).
- Result
    a. Share the outcome and how you specifically contributed to that outcome.
    b. What did you accomplish?
    c. What did you learn?
    d. How did a previous employer benefit from your accomplishment? (e.g., increased sales, lower cost, higher profit, customer satisfaction, fewer injuries)

Examples of Behavioral Questions

- Tell me about a time you had to complete a task with a tight deadline. Describe the situation and how you handled it.
- Describe a time when you had to interact with a difficult client. What was the situation, and how did you handle it?
- What do you do when a team member refuses to complete his or her quota for the work?
- Tell me about a time when you showed initiative on the job.

<u>Preparation for a Specific Interview</u>
- As a Job Hunter, preparing for an interview is specific to a job posting (i.e., job description) from that specific employer for a specific role with that employer.
- Start by making a list of the skills and/or experience that the potential employer referenced in their job posting.
- Consider several examples of past experiences in which you displayed those skills. For each of those experiences, describe the situation, task, action, and result.

<u>Common mistakes answering STAR questions</u>
- Not answering the question
- Not being prepared
- Being too prepared. Keep it light and conversational rather than delivering a story you practiced word-for-word.
- Telling a story that is anything but a success.
- Telling a story that has nothing to do with the question asked. If you are unsure about the question that was asked, ask for clarification before delivering your answer.
- Telling a story that makes you appear unqualified or puts you in a bad light.

<u>Five Interview Tips</u>
1. Be prepared to communicate the impact that you can have on their company. Demonstrate with stories about

past accomplishments and how that impacted past employers.
2. Be specific and quantitative: The STAR method is not about being vague. Communicating metrics has a positive impact. Did you increase sales for your division by 25%? If so, say it with clarity.
3. Be concise: Take the focus off you and your past. What is important to the employer? What is stressing them out? Focus on that.
4. Be honest: No exaggerations.
5. Demonstrate a passion for contributing to the success that is important to their organization.

What are managers looking for?

- Dress the part. Dress like you already work there in the role you're applying for.
- Eye contact: 67% of surveyed hiring managers discounted candidates that had issues making and keeping eye contact.
- Company knowledge: Bring any positive news that you've read about the company. 47% of surveyed hiring managers discount candidates if they don't show that they did company research.
- Confidence: 38% of hiring managers counted people out of the running that didn't smile or show any confidence.
- Life goals: They're looking for people that equate work with meaning and purpose, not just a job.

What questions do you want to ask?
During an interview, there continue to be questions you should be asking the Hiring Manager. Questions like:
- Company culture
- Problems that need to be solved
- Management style
- Expectations for the person they'll hire to fill this position
- Can you thrive and contribute to the success of this organization?

Last impression tips
One last question: to ask the Hiring Manager: "What are the three things you would want me to contribute to the first 100 days on the job that would make you feel like you hired the right person?"
- Wait for an answer
- When you get the answer, respond to the answer with a STAR story followed by saying:
- You are looking for a person to provide ………
- I have done that
- The result for a previous employer was ………
- I can do that for you
- Let him/her/them know your interest level.
- Ask about next steps. What is the timeline for making a hiring decision? When should I get back in touch?

Wrap: "Thanks for your time." "I really enjoyed the talk."

Virtual interviews

- Practice
  a. Practice your video interview skills
  b. Record your practice session to look at body language
  c. Bring a few notes but limit their use
- Environment
  a. Find a space free from stress or anxieties
  b. Clear the background of visual or sound distractions
  c. Need good ambient light plus a lamp behind the computer

- Listen
  a. Let the other person finish speaking.
  b. Jumping in with a verbal response can mute the other person.
  c. Take a moment before providing your answer
- Connect with the Interviewer
  a. Find ways to build rapport. Look for common interest.
  b. Eye contact is important. Look directly into the camera.
  c. Be authentic

Telephone interviews

Exhibit energy during your conversation. You'll naturally show more energy if you stand up with cell phone in hand walking around the room during the interview.
- Speak clearly, enunciate your words, and smile
- Keep background noise to a minimum
- Be an active listener. Attentive.
- Ask insightful questions about the job and the company
- Have all documents available when the call comes in.
- Confirm the interviewer's contact information and spelling of their name.
- Ask about next steps to demonstrate interest in the job.
- Follow-up after a week or two if you haven't heard anything.

Executive Interviews

These comments are specifically directed at individuals that have been in director or officer-level positions in a past employment

and they're looking for an executive level position in the next job.
- Demonstrate that you bring a solution-oriented mindset, resourcefulness, ingenuity, and commitment to the job.
- Look at the interview as a meeting of two people that share the same profound interest in successfully accomplishing the goals of the job.
- Take the focus off yourself. Put the focus on the employer. What is important to them? What do they want? What do they need? What stresses them out.
- Engage with clarity and confidence in a business conversation, where your focus is on the problems that need to be solved – not simply your past.
- Throughout the interview, stay focused on how you are the one that will provide the leadership and creativity to solve their problems. Don't let the interview stay from that subject. They need to be confident that you are the best person for the job.

Interview Tips for Men & Women Over 50

If you are looking for a career change for men over fifty, career change for women over fifty, a new job role for women over fifty or a new job role for men over fifty, it will be helpful if you pay attention to the following interview tips.

1. Open strong
2. Be prepared to answer questions
3. Be a good listener
4. Ask good questions
5. Openly communicate success stories – Keep your stories to 90 seconds or less.
6. Exhibit a warm personality
7. Maintain good eye contact
8. Pay attention to your feelings. Don't let your emotions play a role in your communication.

9. Past disappointments, failed job searches, or resentments toward past employers are a turn-off to a potential hiring manager.
10. If the subject of age comes up, don't get defensive. Be prepared. How will you address age in a positive way if the subject comes up?
11. If you can show an employer that you have the necessary qualifications and you are willing to learn new skills, that will help drown out any perception, fair or not, that you're "too old" for the job.
12. Dress consistent with company dress code for the specific position you're interviewing for.
13. Be prepared with a short list of questions you would like to ask to help you determine whether this is the right job for you.
14. Close strong

Questions to Ponder

(Select all that apply)

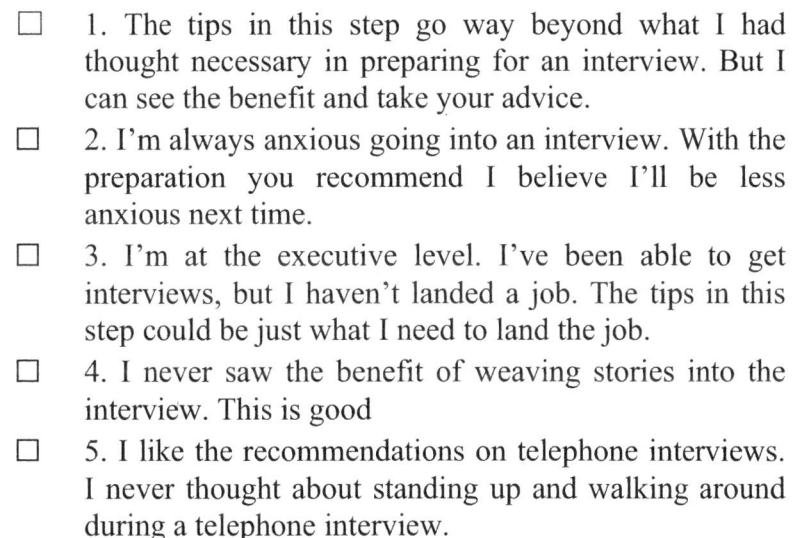

- ☐ 1. The tips in this step go way beyond what I had thought necessary in preparing for an interview. But I can see the benefit and take your advice.
- ☐ 2. I'm always anxious going into an interview. With the preparation you recommend I believe I'll be less anxious next time.
- ☐ 3. I'm at the executive level. I've been able to get interviews, but I haven't landed a job. The tips in this step could be just what I need to land the job.
- ☐ 4. I never saw the benefit of weaving stories into the interview. This is good
- ☐ 5. I like the recommendations on telephone interviews. I never thought about standing up and walking around during a telephone interview.

Secret #10

The Importance of Referrals

You're 14x more likely to land a job through a referral than by applying online. Some experts say it's much higher than that if you're referred to the hiring manager.

Chapter Summary

It's normal to be anxious in the hours leading up to the interview. For the average person, the best answer is to spend considerable time preparing as if you are about to have a face-to-face interview. Then look over the virtual interview and telephone interview tips for those special cases that require additional attention.

Consider the impression you want to make when you first appear in front of the Hiring Manager and any other people he/she has invited to the interview. Think about the STAR stories you want to deliver in response to their behavioral interview questions. Identify the 64 most-likely common questions you'll be asked. Write them down along with the answers you want to communicate. Identify questions you want to ask that will help you determine whether you want to work for that organization and that hiring manager if you receive an offer from them. Think about the impression you want to leave with the last question you ask and other closing remarks you want to make.

Chapter 12 – Interview Follow-Up

> **PSALM 27:13-14** (Living Bible): "*I am expecting the Lord to rescue me again, so that once again I will see his goodness to me here in the land of the living. Don't be impatient. Wait for the Lord, and he will come and save you! Be brave, stouthearted, and courageous. Yes, wait and he will help you.*"

The job transition process is not complete until you have a job offer that you're willing to accept. The Follow-Up after the interview may help in securing the job offer.

- Communicate – Send a thank you by email within 24 hours after the interview. If the interview was with a panel of two or more people, send a personalized thank you to each person, not one email copied to all of them.
- Gratitude – Thank the interviewer and let them know what you are thankful for (e.g., time, information, consideration).
- Reflection – Highlight how your talents align with the role. Choose words that are likely to resonate with their management team.
- Missing – If you forgot to communicate something during the interview, say it in your thank you message.
- Clarification – If you may have misspoken during the interview, clarify your point in your follow-up.
- Confirmation – Restate your interest in the position and the employer and your conviction that you are the right fit for the position.

What if you haven't heard anything for two weeks?
- Call Human Resources or the Hiring Manager to express your continued interest in the position and to inquire about when they'll be deciding.

What if you received a message saying the job was offered to a more qualified candidate?
- Send an email thanking them for their consideration.
- Express continued interest in employment at the company.

JEREMIAH 29:11 (NLT):

"For I know the plans I have for you," says the Lord. "They are plans for good and not for disaster, to give you a future and a hope."

About the Author

It's been my privilege to train and coach many professional adult students that wanted a new career with a fresh start.

I will appreciate any candid feedback you are willing to provide me via email (see last page for email).
- Did this book meet your needs?
- What did you like about this book?
- What improvements would you suggest?

Wrap Up

I thank you for taking the time to go through this material. The job market is complicated. Hiring processes continue to evolve. Follow this training and I believe you will be successful in landing your next job.

Despite the breadth and depth of the training material presented here, you are likely to run into some unique situations where you're not quite sure how to move forward. I want you to be successful in securing that next job in the shortest time possible.

I am offering one-hour coaching sessions to my adult students. The training you'll experience in this eBook is essential. I only offer one-on-one coaching to individuals that have read the book. If you would like to know more about my coaching, please send an email to richard@mynextjob.coach . Explain your situation and why you believe you could benefit from coaching.

This is not a free service, but I know that you will find my one-on-one coaching to be valuable. My training and coaching combined could easily shave four weeks off the time it will take you to secure that next job.

Act now.

Richard Gunderson

The End

Step Up to That New Career

Empower your life with a truly comprehensive approach to changing your career for a fresh start toward a better future.

Career Job Transition LLC

richard@careerjobtransition.com

Made in the USA
Middletown, DE
16 July 2022